TAGINE

Spicy stews from Morocco

TAGINE

Spicy stews from Morocco

RYLAND
PETERS
& SMALL

LONDON NEW YORK

Ghillie Başan

photography by Martin Brigdale

Dedication

For Monica. To shopping in Marrakesh!

Acknowledgments

I would like to thank the team at Ryland Peters & Small:
Alison Starling, for inviting me to write this book, and Liz Sephton
and Ann Baggaley for whipping it into shape. And I am thrilled that
the ever-so-skilled Martin Brigdale took the photographs and, as
always, made each one look stunningly appetizing.

First published in the United States in 2007
by Ryland Peters & Small, Inc
519 Broadway, 5th Floor
New York, NY 10012
www.rylandpeters.com

10

Text © Ghillie Başan 2007
Design and photographs © Ryland Peters & Small 2007

Printed in China

 For digital editions visit
www.rylandpeters.com/apps.php

Library of Congress Cataloging-in-Publication Data

Basan, Ghillie.
    Tagine : spicy stews from Morocco / Ghillie Basan ; photography by Martin
Brigdale.
    p. cm.
    Includes index.
    ISBN 978-1-84597-479-4
    1. Cookery, Moroccan. 2. Stews. I. Title.
    TX725.M8B39 2007
    641.5964--dc22

                                    2007012710

ISBN-10: 1 84597 479 4
ISBN-13: 978 1 84597 479 4

Designer Liz Sephton
Editor Ann Baggaley
Production Gemma Moules
Publishing Director Alison Starling

Food Stylists Bridget Sargeson, Lucy McKelvie
Assistant Food Stylist Stella Sargeson
Stylist Helen Trent
Assistant Stylist Isolde Summerscale
Assistant Photographer Nat Davies
Indexer Hilary Bird

Note
All spoon measurements are level unless otherwise stated.

contents

TAGINE ESSENTIALS

At the heart of an authentic tagine you will find several traditional ingredients that are indispensable if you want to achieve the delightful balance of hot, spicy, sweet, and tart. Most of these ingredients can be found in specialty stores, but it is well worth trying to make some of them at home.

preserved lemons

10 organic, unwaxed lemons
about 10 tablespoons sea salt
freshly squeezed juice of
    3–4 lemons

MAKES 1 LARGE JAR

Added to many dishes as a refreshing, tangy ingredient or garnish, preserved lemons are essential to the cooking of tagines. You can buy jars of ready-preserved lemons in Middle Eastern and African stores, as well as some supermarkets, but it is better to make your own. Be as liberal as you like, tossing them in salads and scattering them over your favorite tagines.

Wash and dry the lemons and slice the ends off each one. Stand each lemon on one end and make two vertical cuts three-quarters of the way through it, as if cutting it into quarters but keeping the base intact. Stuff 1 tablespoon of salt into each lemon, then pack them into a large jar (which has been sterilized by immersion in boiling water and left to drain). Store in a cool place for 3–4 days to soften the lemon skins.

To complete the process, press the lemons down into the jar, so they are even more tightly packed. Pour the freshly squeezed lemon juice over the salted lemons, until they are completely covered. Seal the jar and store it in a cool place for at least 1 month. Rinse the salt off the preserved lemons before using.

harissa

This fiery paste is popular throughout North Africa, served as a condiment or as a dip, or stirred into tagines and couscous to emit its distinct chile taste. This recipe is for the basic paste, to which other ingredients such as fennel, coriander, and mint can be added. Ready-prepared harissa is available in African and Middle Eastern stores, and some supermarkets and gourmet shops.

8 dried red chiles (ancho or New Mexico), seeded
2–3 garlic cloves, chopped
½ teaspoon sea salt
1 teaspoon ground cumin
1 teaspoon ground coriander
¼ cup olive oil

MAKES APPROXIMATELY ¼ CUP (a little harissa goes a long way)

Put the chiles in a bowl and pour over enough warm water to cover them. Let them soak for 1 hour. Drain and squeeze out any excess water. Using a mortar and pestle, pound them to a paste with the garlic and salt (or whizz them in a food processor). Beat in the cumin and coriander and bind with the olive oil.

Store the paste in a sealed jar in the refrigerator with a thin layer of olive oil floating on top. It will keep well for a month.

ras-el-hanout

There is no one recipe for ras-el-hanout, a lovely pungent spice mix, packed with strong Indian aromas of cinnamon, cloves, and ginger combined with local African roots and the delicate, perfumed notes of rosebuds. Every family has its own favorite blend. Some of the spices are available only in the Maghreb, so if your tagine recipe calls for this flavoring your easiest solution is to select one of the ready-prepared spice mixes available in Middle Eastern and African stores. You can also order a moist, aromatic ras-el-hanout online from the spice specialists Zamouri Spices at www.zamourispices.com.

ghee

Ghee (generally known as *samneh* or *samna* in the Arab world), is clarified and evaporated butter. It is sold in cans in Indian, North African and Middle Eastern shops, as well as in some gourmet shops.

To make ghee, simply melt some butter in a heavy-based pan and simmer it until all the water has evaporated, leaving a clear fat with a nutty aroma and taste.

In Morocco, a more pungent clarified butter, *smen*, is made by leaving ghee to mature for several weeks in earthenware pots.

In Arab culture, dates are an age-old source of nutrition and natural sugar; nomads could survive in the desert with dates alone for nourishment. As the fruit is regarded as special, it is often added to festive grain dishes and stews. This slightly sticky date and nut tagine is a favorite at weddings or other family feasts.

lamb tagine with dates, almonds, and pistachios

2–3 tablespoons ghee (see page 9) (or olive oil, plus a pat of butter)

2 onions, finely chopped

1–2 teaspoons ground turmeric

1 teaspoon ground ginger

2 teaspoons ground cinnamon

2¼ lb lean lamb, from the shoulder, neck or leg, cut into bite-size pieces

8 oz moist, ready-to-eat, pitted dates

1 tablespoon dark honey

sea salt and freshly ground black pepper

1 tablespoon olive oil

a pat of butter

2–3 tablespoons blanched almonds

2 tablespoons shelled pistachios

a small bunch of fresh flatleaf parsley, finely chopped

SERVES 4

Heat the ghee in a tagine or heavy-based casserole dish. Stir in the onions and sauté until golden brown. Stir in the turmeric, ginger, and cinnamon. Toss in the meat, making sure it is coated in the spice mixture. Pour in enough water to almost cover the meat and bring it to a boil. Reduce the heat, cover with a lid and simmer gently for roughly 1½ hours.

Add the dates and stir in the honey. Cover with a lid again and simmer for another 30 minutes. Season with salt and lots of black pepper.

Heat the olive oil with the butter in a small pan. Stir in the almonds and pistachios and cook until they begin to turn golden brown. Scatter the nuts over the lamb and dates and sprinkle with the flatleaf parsley. Serve with buttery couscous (see page 60) and a sharp, crunchy salad with preserved lemon (see page 8) to cut the sweetness.

This is a lovely winter dish, decorated with ruby-red pomegranate seeds. Whole, meaty chestnuts are often used in Arab-influenced culinary cultures as a substitute for potatoes. You can use freshly roasted nuts or ready-peeled, vacuum-packed or frozen chestnuts.

lamb tagine with chestnuts, saffron, and pomegranate seeds

2 tablespoons ghee (see page 9)
2 onions, finely chopped
4 garlic cloves, finely chopped
a 1-inch piece of fresh ginger, peeled and finely chopped or shredded
a pinch of saffron threads
1–2 cinnamon sticks
2¼ lb lean lamb, from the shoulder or leg, cut into bite-size pieces
8 oz peeled chestnuts
1–2 tablespoons dark honey
sea salt and freshly ground black pepper
seeds of 1 pomegranate, pith removed
a small bunch of fresh mint leaves, chopped
a small bunch of cilantro leaves, chopped

SERVES 4

Heat the ghee in a tagine or heavy-based casserole dish. Stir in the onions, garlic, and ginger and sauté until they begin to color. Add the saffron and cinnamon sticks, and toss in the lamb. Pour in enough water to almost cover the meat and bring it to a boil. Reduce the heat, cover with a lid, and simmer gently for about 1 hour.

Add the chestnuts and stir in the honey. Cover with the lid again and cook gently for a further 30 minutes, until the meat is very tender. Season to taste with salt and plenty of black pepper and then toss in some of the pomegranate seeds, mint, and cilantro. Sprinkle the remaining pomegranate seeds and herbs over the lamb, and serve with bread or buttery couscous (see page 60).

A classic lamb tagine, sweetened with honey and fruit, is a perfect introduction to the tastes of Morocco. Traditionally, this aromatic dish is served with bread to mop up the syrupy sauce. To balance the sweetness, you could also serve a crunchy salad of shredded carrot, onions, cabbage, and bell peppers, spiked with hot pepper.

lamb tagine with prunes, apricots, and honey

1–2 tablespoons olive oil
2 tablespoons blanched almonds
2 red onions, finely chopped
2–3 garlic cloves, finely chopped
a thumb-size piece of fresh ginger, peeled and chopped
a pinch of saffron threads
2 cinnamon sticks
1–2 teaspoons coriander seeds, crushed
1 lb boned lamb, from the shoulder, leg, or shanks, trimmed and cubed
about 12 pitted prunes, soaked for 1 hour and drained
about 6 dried apricots, soaked for 1 hour and drained
3–4 strips unwaxed orange peel
1–2 tablespoons dark honey
sea salt and freshly ground black pepper
a handful of cilantro leaves, finely chopped

SERVES 4–6

Heat the oil in a tagine or heavy-based casserole dish, stir in the almonds, and cook until they turn golden. Add the onions and garlic and sauté until they begin to color. Stir in the ginger, saffron, cinnamon sticks, and coriander seeds. Toss in the lamb, making sure it is coated in the onion and spices, and sauté for 1–2 minutes.

Pour in enough water to just cover the meat and bring it to a boil. Reduce the heat, cover the tagine or casserole dish and simmer for about 1 hour, until the meat is tender. Add the prunes, apricots, and orange peel, cover the tagine again, and simmer for a further 15–20 minutes. Stir in the honey, season with salt and pepper to taste, cover, and simmer for a further 10 minutes. Make sure there is enough liquid in the pot, as you want the sauce to be syrupy and slightly caramelized, but not dry.

Stir in some of the cilantro and reserve the rest to sprinkle over the top of the dish. Serve immediately with chunks of crusty bread or buttery couscous (see page 60).

Originally from Andalusia, tfaia tagines are popular in northern Morocco, particularly in Tangier. Their trademark is a pungent, nutty flavor that emanates from matured, clarified butter called *smen*—which is an acquired taste for some people. In this recipe, I use ghee, which is ordinary clarified butter.

tfaia tagine with onions, golden almonds, and eggs

1–2 tablespoons ghee (see page 9)
2 garlic cloves, crushed
1 teaspoon ground ginger
1 teaspoon ground coriander
1 teaspoon saffron threads, ground with salt
2¼ lb lamb cutlets
2 onions, finely chopped
6 oz brown Kalamata olives, pitted
2 preserved lemons (see page 8), cut into quarters
sea salt and freshly ground black pepper
a small bunch of cilantro, chopped

TO SERVE:
4 medium or large eggs
½ teaspoon ground saffron, or a pinch of saffron threads
½ tablespoon ghee
2 tablespoons blanched almonds

SERVES 4

Melt the ghee in a tagine or heavy-based casserole dish. Stir in the garlic, ginger, coriander, and saffron, and roll the lamb cutlets in the mixture. Sprinkle the onions over the cutlets and pour in just enough water to cover the meat. Bring the water to a boil, reduce the heat, cover with a lid, and cook gently for about 1½ hours.

Add the olives and lemon quarters and cook, uncovered, for about another 20 minutes to reduce the sauce. Season well with salt and black pepper and toss in the chopped cilantro.

Meanwhile, boil the eggs in their shells for about 4 minutes, so that the yolk is just firm, and shell them. Dissolve the saffron in 2 tablespoons warm water and roll the eggs in the yellow liquid to color them. Cut the eggs in half lengthwise.

In a skillet, melt the ghee and stir in the almonds until golden brown. Sprinkle the almonds over the tagine and arrange the eggs around the edge. Serve immediately with fresh, crusty bread and a leafy salad.

Summer tagines using seasonal vegetables are often quite light and colorful. Other vegetables that might be added to this tagine include tomatoes, eggplant, and peas. This dish is particularly good served with wedges of lemon to squeeze over it, or with finely shredded preserved lemon (see page 8) sprinkled over the top.

summer tagine of lamb, zucchini, bell peppers, and mint

3–4 tablespoons olive oil
1 onion, roughly chopped
4 garlic cloves, roughly chopped
1 teaspoon cumin seeds
1 teaspoon coriander seeds
1 teaspoon dried mint
a 1-inch piece of fresh ginger, peeled and finely chopped or grated
1½ lb lean lamb, cut into bite-size pieces
sea salt and freshly ground black pepper
2 small zucchini, sliced thickly on the diagonal
1 red or green bell pepper, seeded and cut into thick strips
4 tomatoes, peeled, seeded, and cut into chunks
a small bunch of fresh flatleaf parsley, roughly chopped
a small bunch of fresh mint leaves, roughly chopped
1 lemon, cut into quarters, to serve

SERVES 4–6

Heat the olive oil in a tagine or heavy-based casserole dish. Stir in the onion, garlic, cumin and coriander seeds, dried mint, and ginger. Once the onions begin to soften, toss in the meat and pour in enough water to just cover it. Bring the water to a boil, reduce the heat, cover with a lid, and cook gently for about 1½ hours.

Season the cooking juices with salt and pepper. Add the zucchini, bell pepper, and tomatoes, tucking them around the meat (add a little more water if necessary). Cover with a lid again and cook for about 15 minutes, until the zucchini and bell pepper are cooked but retain a bite.

Toss in some of the chopped parsley and fresh mint, sprinkle the rest on top, and serve immediately with lemon wedges to squeeze over the dish.

This summery tagine is best accompanied by a fresh green salad of baby beet greens, spinach, and lettuce leaves.

In this festive dish, a shoulder of lamb is marinated in chermoula—a herb and spice mix—and baked slowly. You can use apples or pears instead of quinces. Buttery couscous (see page 60) or roasted potatoes and a leafy salad are good accompaniments.

baked tagine of lamb with quinces, figs, and honey

3½ lb shoulder of lamb on the bone

2 tablespoons ghee (see page 9)

2 red onions, cut into wedges

8 oz prunes, pitted

8 oz dried figs, or fresh figs, halved

3 tablespoons butter

2 fresh quinces, quartered and cored (keep soaked in water with a squeeze of lemon until ready to use)

2–3 tablespoons orange-flower water

2 tablespoons dark honey

a bunch of fresh flatleaf parsley, chopped

a bunch of cilantro, chopped

FOR THE CHERMOULA:

4 garlic cloves, chopped

a 1½-inch piece of fresh ginger, peeled and chopped

1 red chile, seeded and chopped

1 teaspoon sea salt

a small bunch of cilantro, chopped

a small bunch of fresh flatleaf parsley, chopped

2–3 teaspoons ground coriander

2–3 teaspoons ground cumin

3 tablespoons olive oil

2 tablespoons dark honey

freshly squeezed juice of 1 lemon

SERVES 4–6

First, make the chermoula. Using a mortar and pestle, pound the garlic, ginger, chile, and salt to form a coarse paste. Add the cilantro and parsley and pound into the paste. Beat in the ground coriander and cumin, and bind with the olive oil, honey, and lemon juice (alternatively, you can whizz all the ingredients in an electric blender). Cut small incisions in the shoulder of lamb with a sharp knife and rub the chermoula well into the meat. Cover and leave in the refrigerator for at least 6 hours, or overnight.

Preheat the oven to 350°F.

Heat the ghee in a tagine or heavy-based casserole dish, add the lamb and brown it all over. Transfer the meat to a plate. Stir the onions and any leftover chermoula into the ghee. Add the prunes and if using dried figs add them at this stage. Pour in 1¼ cups water and put the lamb back into the tagine. Cover with the lid and put the tagine in the oven for about 2 hours.

Toward the end of the cooking time, melt the butter in a heavy-based pan, toss in the quinces, and sauté until golden brown. Remove the tagine from the oven and place the golden quince around the meat (if using fresh figs, add them at this stage). Splash the orange-flower water over the lamb and drizzle the honey over the meat and the fruit. Return the tagine to the oven for a further 25–30 minutes, until the meat and fruit are nicely brown and the lamb is so tender it almost falls off the bone. Sprinkle the chopped parsley and cilantro over the top and serve immediately.

Earthy and fruity, with a hint of ginger, this tagine is a good winter warmer. To complete a seasonal meal, you could accompany the dish with roasted pumpkin or butternut squash and couscous (see page 60) tossed with pistachios or pine nuts.

beef tagine with beets and oranges

1–2 tablespoons ghee (see page 9)
3–4 garlic cloves, crushed
1 red onion, halved lengthwise and sliced with the grain
a 1½-inch piece of fresh ginger, peeled and finely chopped or grated
1 red chile, seeded and sliced
2 teaspoons coriander seeds, crushed
2 cinnamon sticks
3–4 beets, peeled and quartered
1 lb lean beef, cut into bite-size cubes or strips
2 thin-skinned oranges, cut into segments
1 tablespoon dark honey
1–2 tablespoons orange-flower water
sea salt and freshly ground black pepper
a pat of butter
2–3 tablespoons shelled pistachio nuts
a small bunch of fresh flatleaf parsley, roughly chopped

SERVES 4–6

Melt the ghee in a tagine or heavy-based casserole dish, and stir in the garlic, onion, and ginger until they begin to color. Add the chile, coriander seeds, and cinnamon sticks. Add the beets and sauté for 2–3 minutes. Toss in the beef and sauté for 1 minute. Pour in enough water to almost cover the beef and beets and bring it to a boil. Reduce the heat, cover with a lid, and simmer for 1 hour, until the meat is very tender.

Add the orange segments, honey, and orange-flower water to the tagine and season the dish with salt and pepper to taste. Cover with the lid and cook for a further 10–15 minutes.

Melt the butter in a small saucepan and toss in the pistachio nuts, stirring them over medium heat until they turn golden brown. Sprinkle them over the tagine along with the flatleaf parsley and serve.

This fairly fiery dish is laced with the powerful flavors and aromas of ras-el-hanout (see page 9), a traditional spice mix. Regional variations use turnip, yam, pumpkin, or butternut squash instead of sweet potatoes. The tagine is best served with plain couscous (see page 60) or chunks of bread and cooling yogurt or a glass of mint tea.

beef tagine with sweet potatoes, peas, ginger, and ras-el-hanout

2 tablespoons ghee (see page 9), or olive oil

a 1½-inch piece of fresh ginger, peeled and finely shredded

1 onion, finely chopped

2¼ lb lean beef, cubed

1–2 teaspoons ras-el-hanout (see page 9)

2 medium sweet potatoes, peeled and cubed

sea salt and freshly ground black pepper

1 lb shelled fresh peas or frozen peas

2–3 tomatoes, peeled, seeded, and chopped

1 preserved lemon (see page 8), finely shredded or chopped

a small bunch of cilantro leaves, finely chopped

SERVES 4

Heat the ghee in a tagine or heavy-based casserole dish. Stir in the ginger and onion and sauté until soft. Toss in the beef and sear it on all sides, then stir in the ras-el-hanout. Pour in enough water to just cover the meat mixture and bring it to a boil. Reduce the heat, cover with the lid, and cook gently for about 40 minutes.

Add the sweet potato to the tagine, season with salt and pepper to taste, cover with the lid, and cook gently for a further 20 minutes, until the meat is tender. Toss in the peas and tomatoes, cover with the lid, and cook for 5–10 minutes.

Sprinkle the preserved lemon and the cilantro over the top and serve.

Variations of this great street dish can be found throughout the Maghreb. It is also often prepared as a snack in the home. In many households, kefta (poached meatballs) are prepared in batches and stored in the refrigerator. Kefta are usually quite fiery, so serve them with bread, parsley, and yogurt to temper their heat.

kefta tagine with eggs and roasted cumin

FOR THE KEFTA:

8 oz ground lamb

1 onion, finely chopped

1 teaspoon dried mint

1–2 teaspoons ras-el-hanout (see page 9)

½ teaspoon cayenne

a small bunch of fresh flatleaf parsley, finely chopped

sea salt and freshly ground black pepper

1 tablespoon butter

¼–½ teaspoon salt

1 teaspoon cayenne pepper or chopped dried chiles

4 medium or large eggs

1–2 teaspoons cumin seeds, dry-roasted and ground

a small bunch of fresh flatleaf parsley, roughly chopped

SERVES 4

To make the kefta, put the ground lamb, onion, mint, ras-el-hanout, cayenne, and parsley in a bowl, season to taste with salt and pepper and mix well together. Using your hands, knead the mixture and mold it into small balls, roughly the size of a shooter marble, so that you end up with about 12 balls.

Fill a tagine or casserole dish with water and bring it to a boil. Carefully drop in the kefta, a few at a time, and poach them for about 10 minutes, turning them so that they are cooked on all sides. Remove them with a slotted spoon and drain on paper towels. Reserve roughly 1¼ cups of the cooking liquid. (If not using the kefta immediately, transfer them to a plate to cool and store in the refrigerator for 2–3 days.)

Add the butter to the reserved cooking liquid in the tagine and bring the mixture to a boil. Stir in the salt and cayenne and drop in the poached kefta. Cook over high heat until almost all the liquid has evaporated. Carefully crack the eggs around the kefta, cover the tagine with a lid, and let the eggs cook in the sauce and steam until they are just set. Sprinkle the roasted cumin seeds and the chopped parsley over the top of the dish. Serve immediately.

Tagines made with meatballs (kefta) do not require long cooking times. Generally, the sauce is prepared first and the meatballs are poached in it, until just cooked. This popular meatball recipe is quite light and lemony and is delicious served with a leafy salad and couscous (see page 60) tossed with hot pepper and herbs.

tagine of spicy kefta with lemon

FOR THE KEFTA:

1 lb finely ground beef or lamb
1 onion, finely chopped or grated
a small bunch of fresh flatleaf parsley, finely chopped
1–2 teaspoons ground cinnamon
1 teaspoon ground cumin
1 teaspoon ground coriander
½ teaspoon cayenne pepper, or 1 teaspoon paprika
sea salt and freshly ground black pepper

1 tablespoon olive oil
1 tablespoon butter or ghee (see page 9)
1 onion, roughly chopped
2–3 garlic cloves, halved and crushed
a thumb-size piece of fresh ginger, peeled and finely chopped
1 red chile, thinly sliced
2 teaspoons ground turmeric
a small bunch of cilantro, roughly chopped
a small bunch of fresh mint leaves, chopped
freshly squeezed juice of 1 lemon
1 lemon, cut into 4 or 6 segments, with pips removed

SERVES 4–6

To make the kefta, pound the ground meat with your knuckles in a bowl. Using your hands, lift up the lump of ground meat and slap it back down into the bowl. Add the onion, parsley, cinnamon, cumin, coriander, and cayenne, and season to taste with salt and black pepper. Using your hands, mix the ingredients together and knead well, pounding the mixture for a few minutes. Take pieces of the mixture and shape them into little walnut-size balls, so that you end up with about 16 kefta. (These can be made ahead of time and kept in the refrigerator for 2–3 days.)

Heat the oil and butter together in a tagine or heavy-based casserole dish. Stir in the onion, garlic, ginger, and chile and sauté until they begin to brown. Add the turmeric and half the cilantro and mint, and pour in roughly 1¼ cups water. Bring the water to a boil, reduce the heat, and simmer, covered, for 10 minutes. Carefully place the kefta in the liquid, cover, and poach the kefta for about 15 minutes, rolling them in the liquid from time to time so they are cooked well on all sides. Pour over the lemon juice, season the liquid with salt, and tuck the lemon segments around the kefta. Poach for a further 10 minutes.

Sprinkle with the remaining cilantro and mint and serve hot.

This is a classic, Spanish-influenced peasant dish, which is often eaten on its own with yogurt and bread but is also served with grilled or roasted meats, such as lamb chops. Either chorizo or merguez sausages can be used, as both impart their spicy flavors to the dish. For a meatless version, just omit the sausage, as the chickpeas are extremely tasty on their own.

chickpea and chorizo tagine
with bay leaves, paprika, and sage

1 cup dried chickpeas, soaked overnight in plenty of water
2–3 tablespoons olive oil
2 red onions, cut in half lengthwise, halved crosswise, and sliced with the grain
2 garlic cloves, chopped
1 thin chorizo, roughly 8 inches long, sliced on the diagonal
2–3 fresh bay leaves
several sprigs of fresh thyme
1–2 teaspoons Spanish smoked paprika
a bunch of fresh sage leaves, shredded
freshly squeezed juice of 1 lemon
sea salt and freshly ground black pepper

SERVES 4

Drain the chickpeas, put them in a large saucepan, and cover with plenty of water. Bring the water to a boil, reduce the heat, and simmer for roughly 45 minutes or until the chickpeas are soft but still have a bite to them. Drain them and refresh under cold running water. Remove any loose skins.

Heat the olive oil in a tagine or heavy-based casserole dish. Stir in the onions and garlic and sauté until they begin to color. Add the chorizo, bay leaves, and thyme and sauté until just brown. Toss in the chickpeas, add the paprika, and cover with a lid. Cook gently for 10–15 minutes, to allow the flavors to mingle.

Toss in the sage leaves and lemon juice. Season with salt and pepper to taste and serve hot with yogurt or flat bread.

Preserved lemon (see page 8) and cracked green olives are two of the principal ingredients of traditional Moroccan cooking. You can buy the olives at Middle Eastern and North African stores and some gourmet shops. The tagine can be made with chicken pieces or a whole chicken. Serve with couscous (see page 60) and salad or vegetables such as steamed carrots tossed with spices and mint.

chicken tagine with preserved lemon, green olives, and thyme

8–10 chicken thighs or 4 whole legs
1 tablespoon olive oil with a pat of butter
2 preserved lemons, cut into strips
6 oz cracked green olives
1–2 teaspoons dried thyme or oregano

FOR THE MARINADE:
1 onion, grated
3 garlic cloves, crushed
a 1-inch piece of fresh ginger, peeled
    and grated
a small bunch of cilantro, finely chopped
a pinch of saffron threads
freshly squeezed juice of 1 lemon
1 teaspoon coarse sea salt
3–4 tablespoons olive oil
sea salt and freshly ground black pepper

SERVES 4

In a bowl, mix together all the ingredients for the marinade. Put the chicken thighs or legs in a shallow dish and coat them in the marinade, rubbing it into the skin. Cover and chill in the refrigerator for 1–2 hours.

Heat the olive oil with the butter in a tagine or heavy-based casserole dish. Remove the chicken pieces from the marinade and brown them in the oil. Pour over the marinade that is left in the dish and add enough water to come halfway up the sides of the chicken pieces. Bring the water to a boil, reduce the heat, cover with a lid, and simmer for about 45 minutes, turning the chicken from time to time.

Add the preserved lemon, olives, and half the thyme to the tagine. Cover again and simmer for a further 15–20 minutes. Check the seasoning and sprinkle the rest of the thyme over the top. Serve immediately from the tagine.

With the tangy notes of preserved lemon (see page 8) combined with sweet grapes, this tagine is deliciously refreshing. It is best accompanied by buttery couscous (see page 60) or flat bread and a leafy salad. You can use ready-prepared artichoke hearts or bottoms, which are available frozen or jarred.

chicken tagine with harissa, artichokes, and green grapes

4 chicken breasts, cut into thick strips or chunks

2 tablespoons olive oil

2 onions, halved lengthwise and sliced with the grain

½ preserved lemon, thinly sliced

1–2 teaspoons sugar

1–2 teaspoons harissa paste (see page 9)

2 teaspoons tomato paste

1¼ cups chicken stock or water

1 x 13-oz jar artichoke hearts, drained, rinsed, and halved

about 16 fresh green grapes, halved lengthwise

a bunch of cilantro leaves, coarsely chopped

sea salt and freshly ground black pepper

FOR THE MARINADE:

2 garlic cloves, crushed

1 teaspoon ground turmeric

freshly squeezed juice of 1 lemon

1 tablespoon olive oil

SERVES 4

First, make the marinade. In a bowl, mix together the garlic, turmeric, lemon juice, and olive oil. Toss the chicken in the mixture, then cover and leave in the refrigerator to marinate for 1–2 hours.

Heat the oil in a tagine or heavy-based casserole dish. Stir in the onions, preserved lemon, and the sugar and sauté for 2–3 minutes, until slightly caramelized. Toss in the marinated chicken, then add the harissa and tomato pastes. Pour in the stock and bring it to a boil. Reduce the heat, cover with a lid, and cook gently for 15 minutes.

Toss in the artichoke hearts, cover with the lid again, and cook for a further 5 minutes. Add the grapes with some of the cilantro and season to taste with salt and pepper. Sprinkle with the remaining cilantro to serve.

This tagine is both fruity and spicy, and the rosemary and ginger give it a delightful aroma. It can be made with chicken pieces, pheasant, or duck, and needs only a buttery couscous (see page 60) and a leafy salad to accompany it.

spicy chicken tagine with apricots, rosemary, and ginger

2 tablespoons olive oil with a pat of butter
1 onion, finely chopped
3 sprigs of rosemary, 1 finely chopped, the other 2 cut in half
a 1½-inch piece of fresh ginger, peeled and finely chopped
2 red chiles, seeded and finely chopped
1–2 cinnamon sticks
8 chicken thighs
¾ cup dried apricots
2 tablespoons clear honey
1 x 14-oz can plum tomatoes with their juice
sea salt and freshly ground black pepper
a small bunch of fresh green or purple basil leaves

SERVES 4

Heat the oil and butter in a tagine or heavy-based casserole dish. Stir in the onion, chopped rosemary, ginger, and chiles and sauté until the onion begins to soften. Stir in the halved rosemary sprigs and the cinnamon sticks. Add the chicken thighs and brown them on both sides. Toss in the apricots with the honey, then stir in the plum tomatoes with their juice. (Add a little water if necessary, to ensure there is enough liquid to cover the base of the tagine and submerge the apricots.) Bring the liquid to a boil, then reduce the heat. Cover with a lid and cook gently for 35–40 minutes.

Season to taste with salt and pepper. Shred the larger basil leaves and leave the small ones intact. Sprinkle them over the chicken and serve the dish immediately.

This traditional Moorish dish appears in various guises throughout the Arab-influenced world. Poultry cooked with dates and honey is probably one of the most ancient culinary combinations and the finished dish is deliciously succulent. You can substitute the duck with chicken, Rock Cornish hens, or poussins, if you prefer.

tagine of duck breasts with dates, honey, and orange-flower water

a 1-inch piece of fresh ginger, peeled and chopped
2–3 garlic cloves, chopped
2–3 tablespoons olive oil with a pat of butter
2 cinnamon sticks
4 duck breasts on the bone
2–3 tablespoons clear honey
1 cup moist, pitted dates
1–2 tablespoons orange-flower water
sea salt and freshly ground black pepper

TO SERVE:
1 tablespoon butter
2–3 tablespoons blanched almonds

SERVES 4

Using a mortar and pestle, pound the ginger and garlic to a paste. Heat the olive oil and butter in a tagine or heavy-based casserole dish, then stir in the ginger–garlic paste and the cinnamon sticks. Once the mixture begins to color, add the duck breasts and brown the skin.

Stir in the honey and tuck the dates around the duck. Add enough water (the amount will vary according to the size of your tagine) to cover the base of the tagine and to come about one-third of the way up the duck breasts. Bring the water to a boil, reduce the heat, and cover with a lid. Cook gently for about 25 minutes.

Add the orange-flower water and season to taste with salt and pepper. Cover and cook for a further 5 minutes, or until the duck is tender.

In a skillet, melt the butter and stir in the almonds. Sauté until golden brown and then scatter them over the duck. Serve immediately with a mound of couscous (see page 60), flavored with lemon and herbs.

FISH AND SHELLFISH TAGINES

Baking whole fish in a tagine keeps the flesh deliciously moist. Obviously, you need to select fish that fits snugly into your tagine. The most popular fish for oven-baking in North Africa include red mullet, sardines, red snapper, grouper, and sea bass. You could serve this dish with couscous (see page 60) or a tangy salad.

oven-baked tagine of red mullet, tomatoes, and lime

2 tablespoons olive oil
2 tablespoons butter
2–3 garlic cloves, thinly sliced
3–4 good-size red mullet or 3–4 small red snapper, gutted and cleaned
sea salt
2–3 large tomatoes, thinly sliced
1 lime, thinly sliced

TO SERVE:
a small bunch of fresh flatleaf parsley, coarsely chopped
1 lime, cut into wedges

SERVES 3–4

Preheat the oven to 350°F.

Heat the olive oil and butter in a tagine or ovenproof dish. Stir in the garlic and sauté until it begins to brown. Put the fish in the tagine and cook it until the skin is brown and has lightly buckled. (If you are using an ovenproof dish, you can brown the garlic and fish in a frying pan first.) Turn off the heat, sprinkle a little salt over the fish, and tuck the slices of tomato and lime over and around them. Cover with the lid and cook in the oven for about 15 minutes.

Remove the lid and bake for a further 5–10 minutes, until the fish is cooked and nicely brown on top (you can do this under the broiler, if you prefer).

Sprinkle the parsley over the top and serve with wedges of lime to squeeze over the fish.

The fish tagines of coastal Morocco are often made with whole fish, or with large chunks of fleshy fish such as sea bass, monkfish, and cod. The fish is first marinated in the classic chermoula flavoring, and the dish is given an additional fillip with a little white wine or sherry. Serve with new potatoes and a leafy salad.

fish tagine with preserved lemon and mint

2 lb fresh fish fillets, such as cod or haddock, cut into large chunks

2–3 tablespoons olive oil

1 red onion, finely chopped

2 carrots, finely chopped

2 celery ribs, finely chopped

1 preserved lemon (see page 8), finely chopped

1 x 14-oz can of plum tomatoes with their juice

⅔ cup fish stock or water

⅔ cup white wine or fino sherry

sea salt and freshly ground black pepper

a bunch of fresh mint leaves, finely shredded

FOR THE CHERMOULA:

2–3 garlic cloves, chopped

1 red chile, seeded and chopped

1 teaspoon sea salt

a small bunch of cilantro

a pinch of saffron threads

1–2 teaspoons ground cumin

3–4 tablespoons olive oil

freshly squeezed juice of 1 lemon

SERVES 4–6

First, make the chermoula. Using a mortar and pestle, pound the garlic and chile with the salt to form a paste. Add the cilantro leaves and pound to a coarse paste. Beat in the saffron threads and cumin and bind well with the olive oil and lemon juice (you can whizz all the ingredients together in an electric blender, if you prefer). Reserve 2 teaspoons of the mixture for cooking. Toss the fish chunks in the remaining chermoula, cover, and marinate in the refrigerator for 1–2 hours.

Heat the oil in a tagine or heavy-based casserole dish. Stir in the onion, carrots, and celery and sauté until softened. Add the preserved lemon (reserving a little for sprinkling) with the reserved 2 teaspoons of chermoula and the tomatoes and stir in well. Cook gently for about 10 minutes to reduce the liquid, then add the stock and the wine. Bring the liquid to a boil, cover the tagine, reduce the heat, and simmer for 10–15 minutes.

Toss the fish in the tagine, cover, and cook gently for 6–8 minutes, until the fish is cooked through. Season to taste with salt and pepper, sprinkle with the reserved preserved lemon and the shredded mint leaves, and serve immediately.

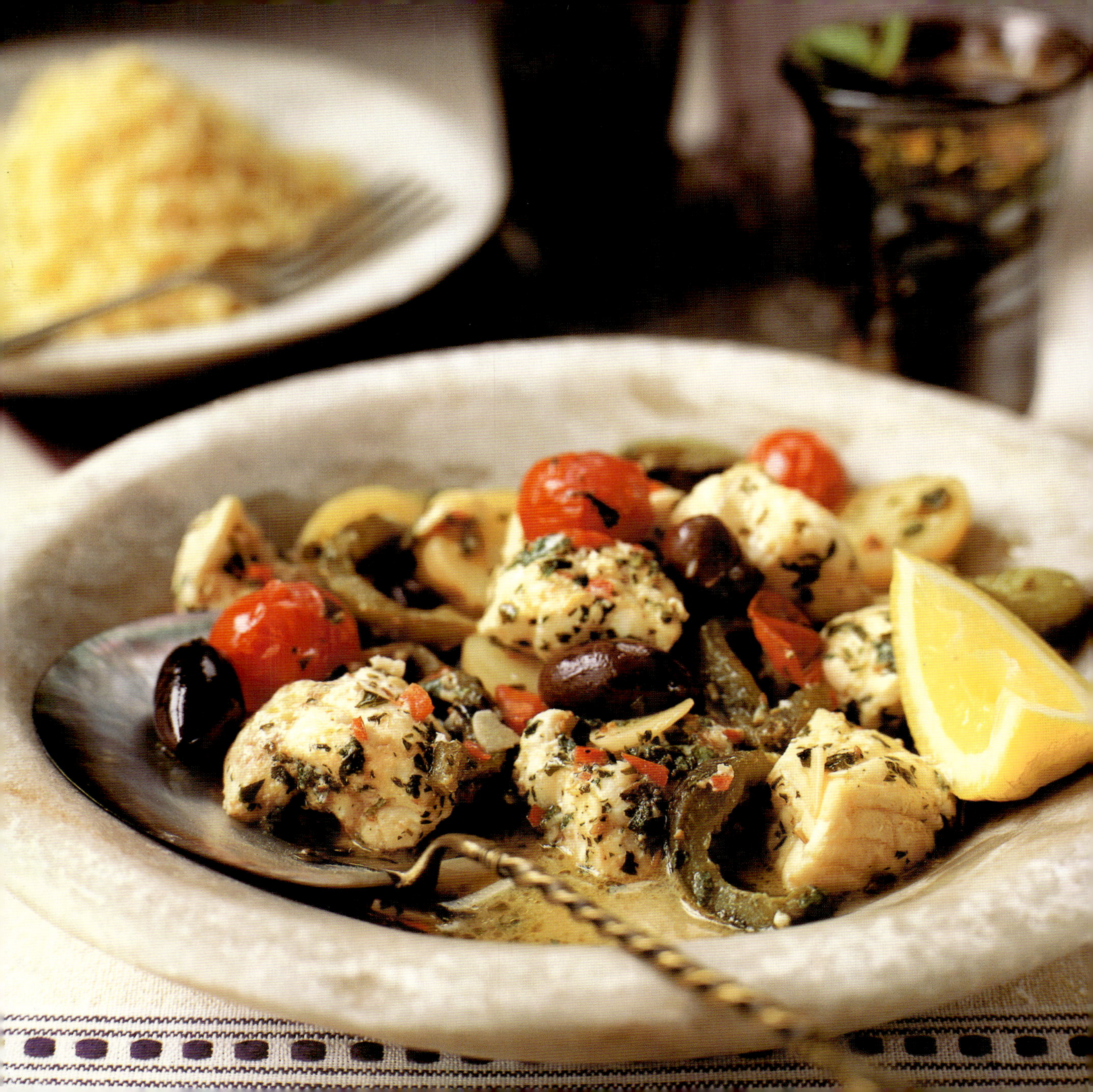

For this lovely tagine, flavored with garlic, chile, cumin, and cilantro (a popular version of Morocco's favorite chermoula spice mix), you can used any meaty white fish. Serve it as a meal in itself with chunks of fresh, crusty bread to mop up the delicious juices, or with buttery couscous (see page 60).

tagine of monkfish, potatoes, cherry tomatoes, and black olives

about 2 lb monkfish tail, cut
    into chunks
about 12 small new potatoes
3 tablespoons olive oil with a pat
    of butter
3–4 garlic cloves, thinly sliced
12–16 cherry tomatoes
2 green bell peppers, broiled until black,
    peeled, and cut into strips
sea salt and freshly ground black pepper
about 12 fleshy black olives
1 lemon, cut into wedges, to serve

FOR THE CHERMOULA:
2 garlic cloves
1 teaspoon coarse salt
1–2 teaspoons cumin seeds, crushed
    or ground
1 red chile, seeded and chopped
freshly squeezed juice of 1 lemon
2 tablespoons olive oil
a small bunch of cilantro,
    roughly chopped

SERVES 4–6

First, make the chermoula. Using a mortar and pestle, pound the garlic with the salt to a smooth paste. Add the cumin, chile, lemon juice, and olive oil and stir in the cilantro. Put the fish in a shallow dish and rub it with most of the chermoula (reserve a little for cooking). Cover and marinate in the refrigerator for 1–2 hours.

Meanwhile, bring a saucepan of water to a boil and drop in the potatoes. Boil vigorously for about 8 minutes to soften them a little, then drain and refresh under cold running water. Peel and cut them in half lengthwise.

Heat 2 tablespoons olive oil with the butter in a tagine or heavy-based saucepan. Stir in the garlic and, when it begins to brown, add the tomatoes to soften them. Add the skinned peppers and the reserved chermoula, and season to taste with salt and pepper. Tip the mixture onto a plate.

Arrange the potatoes over the base of the tagine and spoon half of the tomato and pepper mixture over them. Place the chunks of marinated fish on top and spoon the rest of the tomato and pepper mixture over the fish. Tuck the olives in and around the fish and drizzle the remaining tablespoon of olive oil over the top. Pour in roughly ½ cup of water and check the seasoning. Cover with a lid and steam for 15–20 minutes, until the fish is cooked through. Serve immediately with lemon wedges.

In some coastal areas of Morocco, such as Casablanca and Tangier, restaurants offer shellfish tagines—a modern specialty, rather than a traditional one. Whether these dishes are the result of colonial French influence or simply devised for the tourists, they are certainly very tasty. They are best appreciated on their own, with chunks of crusty bread to mop up the creamy sauce.

creamy shellfish tagine with fennel and harissa

1 lb fresh mussels in their shells, scrubbed clean and rinsed
1 lb shrimp in their shells, thoroughly rinsed
freshly squeezed juice of 1 lemon
2 tablespoons olive oil
4–6 shallots, finely chopped
1 fennel bulb, chopped
1–2 teaspoons harissa paste (see page 9)
⅔ cup cream
sea salt and freshly ground black pepper
a generous bunch of cilantro, finely chopped

SERVES 4–6

Put the mussels and shrimp in a wide saucepan with just enough water to cover them. Add the lemon juice, cover the pan, and bring the liquid to a boil. Shake the pan and cook the shellfish for about 3 minutes, until the shells of the mussels have opened. Drain the shellfish, reserve the liquor, and discard any mussels that have not opened. Refresh the mussels and shrimp under cold running water and shell most of them (you can, of course, leave them all in their shells if you prefer, as long as you are prepared for messy eating).

Heat the olive oil in a tagine or heavy-based casserole dish. Stir in the shallots and fennel and sauté until soft. Stir in the harissa and pour in 1¼ cups of the reserved cooking liquor. Bring the liquid to a boil and continue to boil for 2–3 minutes, reduce the heat, and stir in the cream. Simmer gently for about 5 minutes to let the flavors mingle, season to taste with salt and lots of black pepper, and stir in the mussels and shrimp. Toss in half of the cilantro, cover with a lid, and cook gently for about 5 minutes. Sprinkle the remaining cilantro over the top and serve immediately.

Substantial enough for a main meal, served with couscous (see page 60) and yogurt, vegetable tagines also make good side dishes for grilled or roasted meats or other tagines. You can cook this one in the oven if you like, using the tagine base or an ovenproof pan.

tagine of butternut squash, shallots, raisins, and almonds

3 tablespoons olive oil with a pat of butter
about 12 pink shallots, peeled and left whole
about 8 garlic cloves, lightly crushed
⅔ cup golden raisins
⅔ cup blanched almonds
1–2 teaspoons harissa paste (see page 9)
2 tablespoons dark honey
1 medium butternut squash, halved lengthwise, peeled, seeded, and sliced
sea salt and freshly ground black pepper
a small bunch of cilantro leaves, finely chopped
1 lemon, cut into quarters, to serve

SERVES 3–4

Heat the oil and butter in a tagine or heavy-based casserole dish. Stir in the shallots and garlic and sauté them until they begin to color. Add the raisins and almonds and stir in the harissa and honey. Toss in the squash, making sure it is coated in the spicy oil. Pour in enough water to cover the base of the tagine and cover with the lid. Cook gently for 15–20 minutes, until the shallots and squash are tender but still quite firm.

Season to taste with salt and pepper, sprinkle the cilantro leaves over the top, and serve with wedges of lemon to squeeze over the dish.

You can make this hearty country dish with either fresh or frozen artichokes. If using fresh, you must first remove the outer leaves, then cut off the stems and scoop out the choke and hairy bits with a teaspoon. Rub the artichokes with lemon juice or place in a bowl of cold water with lemon juice to prevent discoloration.

tagine of artichokes, potatoes, peas, and saffron

2–3 tablespoons olive oil
2 red onions, halved lengthwise, cut in half crosswise, and sliced with the grain
4 garlic cloves, crushed
2 teaspoons coriander seeds
1 teaspoon cumin seeds
2 teaspoons ground turmeric
1–2 teaspoons dried mint
8 medium boiling potatoes, peeled and quartered
1½ cups vegetable or chicken stock
4 prepared artichokes, quartered
a small bunch of cilantro leaves, chopped
1½ cups shelled fresh peas or frozen peas
½ preserved lemon (see page 8), finely shredded
sea salt and freshly ground black pepper
a small bunch of fresh mint leaves, to serve

SERVES 4–6

Heat the olive oil in a tagine or heavy-based casserole dish, add the onion, and sauté until it begins to soften. Add the garlic, coriander and cumin seeds, ground turmeric, and the dried mint. Toss in the potatoes, coating them in the spices. Pour in the stock and bring it to a boil. Reduce the heat, cover with a lid, and cook gently for about 10 minutes.

Toss in the artichokes and cilantro and cook for a further 5 minutes. Stir in the peas and preserved lemon, and season to taste with salt and pepper. Cook gently for 5–10 minutes, uncovered, until the artichokes are tender and the liquid has reduced.

Sprinkle with the fresh mint leaves and serve with couscous (see page 60) or chunks of fresh, crusty bread.

This syrupy, caramelized tagine is delicious served as a main dish, with couscous (see page 60) and a herby salad, or as a side dish to accompany grilled or roasted meats. Sweet potatoes, butternut squash, and pumpkin can be used instead of true yams.

tagine of yam, shallots, carrots, and prunes

2–3 tablespoons olive oil with a pat of butter

a 1½-inch piece of fresh ginger, peeled and finely chopped or grated

1–2 cinnamon sticks or 1–2 teaspoons ground cinnamon

about 16 small shallots, peeled and left whole

1¾ lb yam, peeled and cut into bite-size chunks

2 medium carrots, peeled and cut into bite-size chunks

¾ cup pitted prunes

1 tablespoon dark honey

2 cups vegetable or chicken stock

a small bunch of cilantro leaves, roughly chopped

a few fresh mint leaves, chopped

sea salt and freshly ground black pepper

SERVES 4–6

Heat the olive oil and butter in a tagine or heavy-based casserole dish, and stir in the ginger and cinnamon sticks. Toss in the shallots and when they begin to color add the yam and the carrots. Sauté for 2–3 minutes, then add the prunes and the honey. Pour in the stock and bring it to a boil. Reduce the heat, cover with a lid, and cook gently for about 25 minutes.

Remove the lid and stir in some of the cilantro and mint. Season to taste with salt and pepper and reduce the liquid, if necessary, by cooking for a further 2–3 minutes without the lid. The vegetables should be tender and slightly caramelized in a very syrupy sauce. Sprinkle with the remaining cilantro and mint and serve immediately.

As lima beans are so meaty, this tagine can be served as a main dish, but it is also excellent as an accompaniment to grilled or roasted meats and poultry. Bean dishes like this vary from region to region in Morocco, sometimes spiked with chiles or hot chorizo-style sausages.

tagine of lima beans, cherry tomatoes, and black olives

1 cup dried lima beans, soaked overnight in plenty of water

2–3 tablespoons olive oil with a pat of butter

4 garlic cloves, halved and crushed

2 red onions, halved lengthwise, cut in half crosswise, and sliced with the grain

1–2 red or green chiles, seeded and thinly sliced

1–2 teaspoons coriander seeds, crushed

a 1-inch piece of fresh ginger, peeled and finely shredded or chopped

a pinch of saffron threads

about 16–20 cherry tomatoes

1–2 teaspoons sugar

1–2 teaspoons dried thyme

2–3 tablespoons black olives, pitted

freshly squeezed juice of 1 lemon

sea salt and freshly ground black pepper

a small bunch of flatleaf parsley, coarsely chopped

SERVES 4–6

Drain and rinse the soaked beans. Put them in a deep saucepan with plenty of water and bring to a boil. Boil for about 5 minutes, then reduce the heat and simmer gently for about 1 hour, or until the beans are tender but not mushy. Drain and refresh them under cold running water.

Heat the olive oil and butter in a tagine or heavy-based casserole dish. Stir in the garlic, onions, and chiles and sauté until they begin to soften. Add the coriander seeds, ginger, and saffron. Cover and cook gently for 4–5 minutes. Toss in the tomatoes with the sugar and thyme, cover with the lid again, and cook until the skin on the tomatoes begins to crinkle.

Toss in the beans and olives, pour over the lemon juice, and season to taste with salt and pepper. Cover with the lid and cook gently for about 5 minutes, until the beans and olives are heated through. Sprinkle with the flatleaf parsley and serve with chunks of crusty bread and a dollop of thick, creamy yogurt, if liked.

This vegetarian tagine is best made with baby eggplants, but you can also use slender, larger eggplants cut into quarters lengthwise. As a main dish, it is delicious served with couscous (see page 60), or bulgur, and a dollop of thick, creamy yogurt; it can also be served as a side dish to accompany meat or poultry.

tagine of baby eggplants with cilantro and mint

1–2 tablespoons olive oil
1 tablespoon butter or ghee (see page 9)
1–2 red onions, halved lengthwise and
    sliced with the grain
3–4 garlic cloves, crushed
1–2 red chiles, seeded and sliced, or
    2–3 dried red chiles, left whole
1–2 teaspoons coriander seeds, roasted
    and crushed
1–2 teaspoons cumin seeds, roasted
    and crushed
2 teaspoons sugar
16 baby eggplants, with stalks intact
2 x 14-oz cans of chopped tomatoes
sea salt and freshly ground black pepper
a bunch of fresh mint leaves,
    roughly chopped
a bunch of cilantro, roughly chopped

SERVES 4

Heat the oil and butter in a tagine or heavy-based casserole dish. Stir in the onions and garlic and sauté until they begin to color. Add the chiles, the coriander and cumin seeds, and the sugar. When the seeds give off a nutty aroma, toss in the whole baby eggplants, coating them in the onion and spices. Tip in the tomatoes, cover with a lid, and cook gently for about 40 minutes, until the eggplants are beautifully tender.

Season to taste with salt and pepper and add half the mint and cilantro leaves. Cover and simmer for a further 5–10 minutes. Sprinkle with the remaining mint and cilantro leaves and serve hot.

This country-style dish is vegetarian, typical of regions where meat is regarded as a luxury by most families. Legumes of all kinds and, in particular, chickpeas, provide the nourishing content of these dishes. To avoid lengthy preparation and cooking, use canned chickpeas. For simple accompaniments, offer yogurt or bread.

spicy carrot and chickpea tagine with turmeric and cilantro

3–4 tablespoons olive oil
1 onion, finely chopped
3–4 garlic cloves, finely chopped
2 teaspoons ground turmeric
1–2 teaspoons cumin seeds
1 teaspoon ground cinnamon
½ teaspoon cayenne pepper
½ teaspoon ground black pepper
1 tablespoon dark honey
3–4 medium carrots, sliced on
   the diagonal
2 x 14½-oz cans of chickpeas, thoroughly
   rinsed and drained
sea salt
1–2 tablespoons rosewater
a bunch of cilantro leaves, finely chopped
1 lemon, cut into wedges, to serve

SERVES 4

Heat the oil in a tagine or heavy-based casserole dish, add the onion and garlic, and sauté until soft. Add the turmeric, cumin, cinnamon, cayenne, black pepper, honey, and carrots. Pour in enough water to cover the base of the tagine and cover with a lid. Cook gently for 10–15 minutes.

Toss in the chickpeas, check that there is still enough liquid at the base of the tagine, cover with the lid, and cook gently for a further 5–10 minutes. Season with salt, sprinkle the rosewater and cilantro leaves over the top, and serve with lemon wedges.

index

conversion chart

Weights and measures have been rounded up
or down slightly to make measuring easier.

Measuring butter:
A US stick of butter weighs 4 oz which is
approximately 115 g or 8 tablespoons. The recipes
in this book require the following conversions:

American	Metric	Imperial
6 tbsp	85 g	3 oz
7 tbsp	100 g	3½ oz
1 stick	115 g	4 oz

Volume equivalents:

American	Metric	Imperial
1 teaspoon	5 ml	
1 tablespoon	15 ml	
¼ cup	60 ml	2 fl oz
⅓ cup	75 ml	2½ fl oz
½ cup	125 ml	4 fl oz
⅔ cup	150 ml	5 fl oz (¼ pint)
¾ cup	175 ml	6 fl oz
1 cup	250 ml	8 fl oz

Weight equivalents:

Imperial	Metric
1 oz	30 g
2 oz	55 g
3 oz	85 g
3½ oz	100 g
4 oz	115 g
6 oz	175 g
8 oz (½ lb)	225 g
9 oz	250 g
10 oz	280 g
12 oz	350 g
13 oz	375 g
14 oz	400 g
15 oz	425 g
16 oz (1 lb)	450 g

Measurements:

Inches	cm
¼ inch	5 mm
½ inch	1 cm
1 inch	2.5 cm
2 inches	5 cm
3 inches	7 cm
4 inches	10 cm
5 inches	12 cm
6 inches	15 cm
7 inches	18 cm
8 inches	20 cm
9 inches	23 cm
10 inches	25 cm
11 inches	28 cm
12 inches	30 cm

Oven temperatures:

120°C	(250°F)	Gas ½
140°C	(275°F)	Gas 1
150°C	(300°F)	Gas 2
170°C	(325°F)	Gas 3
180°C	(350°F)	Gas 4
190°C	(375°F)	Gas 5
200°C	(400°F)	Gas 6